A Spiritual Mystery In 7 Episodes

Dr. Jim Turrell

A Spiritual Mystery in 7 Episodes

First Edition
©2025 Dr. Jim Turrell
All rights reserved
HeartTalk
ISBN 978-0-9667986-7-8

This book is copyrighted. No portion of this book may be copied or distributed in any form, print, electronic, or any other method in current or future use without the express written permission of the author.

Dedicated to Tom Engle

Table of Contents

Episode 1   The Lens Of New Beginnings 1
Episode 2   The Treasure of Peace 11
Episode 3   The Bridge of Friendship 19
Episode 4   The Fire of Love 29
Episode 5   The Crown of Health 43
Episode 6   The Feast of Joy 55
Episode 7   The Kingdom of Prosperity 69

Episode 1
The Lens Of New Beginnings

Anna lifted the lid of her father's trunk with the kind of anticipation reserved for old maps and forbidden treasure. The hinges groaned as if reluctant to yield, and dust curled upward like incense from a hidden altar. The faint tang of cedar and iron filled her lungs. Her pulse quickened. Surely there would be relics—something to tell her who he had been, and by reflection, who she was meant to become.

But as her hands sifted through yellowed envelopes, brittle photographs, tarnished buckles, the faint crumble of moth-eaten cloth, she felt only the ache of disappointment. Her fingers traced emptiness disguised as remnants. And then—there it was. Not gold. Not heirloom. Not anything she could explain.

A cracked lens.

Its rim was dented, its glass fractured into jagged constellations, as if the night sky itself had fallen and shattered.

Her shoulders sagged. This was no inheritance. No treasure. Just the kind of useless relic left behind when someone forgets to empty the drawer. She almost dropped it back into the trunk, letting it fall again into obscurity. But in the hush of that moment, a voice pressed against her ear—not loud, but undeniable: *Look again.*

Reluctantly, she lifted the lens. It caught the waning light in broken rays, shimmering like a dying star clinging to its last fire. She pressed it to her eye, half mocking her own obedience to a whisper.

Through its fractured pane, the ordinary street outside transformed.

The cracked sidewalks stretched into rivers of chalk galaxies, drawn by children whose hands were powdered in cosmic dust. Their laughter was not ordinary laughter—it was the kind that unlatched invisible doors, ringing like bells in a hidden cathedral. The houses—once dull and identical—leaned forward as if listening. The flowers bent low over fences, not from weight but with the urgency of proclamation, whispering: *Wake up. Beauty lives here.*

Her chest tightened. She blinked once, twice. But the vision held. The world beyond the lens quivered with meaning. It wasn't the street that had changed—it was her eyes. And she realized, with a cold clarity, that she hadn't been living at all. She had only been enduring, trudging through days blind to the symphony humming at the edges.

Her father's voice returned, remembered yet strangely immediate: *The eyes you use decide the world you see.*

The lens warmed in her hand, pulsing like a heartbeat. Three words pressed into her mind—alive, insistent, unshakable: **Perception. Possibility. Presence.** They were less instruction than incantation, keys that turned locks she had not known were there.

And then, as if summoned by those words, the children's galaxies swirled wider. Figures appeared—one, a rabbi in plain clothes, smiling with the ease of someone who carried eternity in His pockets. Beside Him stood a man with dusty hands, the kind of dust that comes from unnoticed kindness, the residue of service. Their presence carried no announcement, yet the air bent toward them as reeds bend toward a river's flow.

The rabbi looked at the lens in her hand. His voice carried the tone of dawn itself. "New begins when you learn to look again."

His companion chuckled, recalling. "We once counted five loaves and two fish and called it *not enough*. But He showed us to see again. And not enough became a feast."

Anna clutched the lens. Its cracks shimmered like veins of light. Brokenness had never looked so whole.

Later, when she told her brother, he laughed until tears streaked his face. "Figures. Dad always left things half-fixed. Even your inheritance came pre-broken." They both laughed—wet, awkward, aching laughter. And in that unlikely moment, grief loosened. Humor had slipped in, resurrection sneaking through the side door.

That night, shadows pressed close and silence held her like a cloak. Anna sat with her journal, words scratching onto the page before she could stop them: *If I've missed this much beauty on my own street, what else have I missed in my life?*

As the ink dried, the lens flickered faintly. Light seemed to map itself inside the cracks, a constellation of pathways stretching toward horizons unseen.

She closed her eyes and almost slept. But when she opened them again, the glow had softened into something stranger: beside the lens lay a folded envelope, pale as bone, sealed with no wax, bearing no name. She had not placed it there. She had not seen it before.

Anna reached for it, her fingers trembling. Moonlight slipped across the desk as though it, too, leaned closer. She turned the envelope over— blank, silent, impenetrable. She felt the weight of a message not yet spoken. She had not broken the seal, yet a meaning opened anyway, as if the letter spoke without words.

It was less paper than invitation—a quiet map inked in silence, leading to a door without a keyhole.

She pressed it to her chest. A stillness moved through her bones. She did not hear the word, yet it lingered in her marrow: *Peace.*

The next morning, unsettled, she carried both lens and letter to Rev. Jim. She set them before him. The lens caught the light like fire frozen in glass. The envelope sat mute, unreadable, yet heavy with presence.

She whispered, "This looks broken. And this looks empty. How can I see anything good through things like these?"

He held the lens gently, then laid his hand over the envelope as though consecrating it. His eyes gleamed with something more than sight. "Sometimes," he said, "the clearest visions come through the cracks. And sometimes the truest letters carry no ink. The broken and the blank—they are not barriers, Anna. They are windows. Openings where divine light and divine silence enter."

She frowned, hesitant. "So I can choose to see differently, even with all this damage… even with all this emptiness?"

"Yes," he said firmly. "Perception is the sacred key. The past does not change—but the way you see it does. And when vision shifts, possibility appears. Even emptiness is not wasted; it is the page where revelation waits."

The lens grew warm in her palms. The letter, still unopened, seemed to breathe. For the first time, she wondered if both had chosen her.

She whispered, almost afraid, "Maybe I've been holding the wrong vision. Maybe the cracks are how the light gets through. And maybe the silence is how peace arrives."

Rev. Jim smiled. "Exactly. Sometimes the map to wholeness is already in your hands. You just need the courage to see differently."

Her heart steadied. Yet the mystery deepened. Because she knew—the lens was never about glass, the letter never about ink. They were about her eyes, her heart, her willingness to trust what could not yet be seen.

And in that realization, words welled up, rising like a song, spilling like poetry:

🎤 Slam Poem

He left me nothing—

just a cracked lens.

I almost tossed it,

till it whispered: *Look again.*

Through it,

streets turned sacred, laughter healed, flowers preached.

And I knew—I hadn't been living. I'd been surviving.

The night ended with a song, soft but insistent, drifting like a hymn remembered from childhood. She sang it to herself, and the cracked lens seemed to hum along, while the unopened letter lay still, glowing faintly in the dark.

🎵 Closing Refrain (to the melody of *Morning Has Broken*)

Morning has broken, like the first morning.

Hope has awoken, life is reborn.

Lift up your vision, courage is rising

See with new eyes, the day is restored.

Moonlight folded across the room like an unopened letter. She broke no seal, yet a meaning opened anyway

a quiet map inked in silence, leading to a door without a keyhole.

Behind it, something waited that did not argue, did not hurry.

And though she could not yet name it, her spirit felt its shape:

a treasure sealed not in gold,

but in the hush of stillness itself—**Peace.**

✸ *Every new beginning starts with the courage to see differently. But vision is only the first key. For beyond sight, the journey demands the heart to rest, to anchor in the treasure hidden beneath noise*

Episode 2
The Treasure of Peace

Anna's journey began the day she opened her father's trunk. She had expected letters, journals, or some confession to explain the silence he left behind. Instead, there was only a cracked lens. At first it felt like failure, like one more mystery he had taken with him. But in time, the lens became something else—a key, a doorway. Her father had been a student of Emerson, who taught that the eye is the first circle and the horizon the second, and throughout life we are invited to see further, wider. Anna had dismissed those words in her youth. And though she had studied Ernest Holmes, she had never understood him either. His teachings about mirrors and consciousness felt abstract—until her father died. Only then, with grief as her teacher, did the broken lens begin to speak. It whispered that while the past cannot change, how we see it can.

That truth accompanied her into the marketplace one morning. She entered as though stepping into a memory she had never wanted to revisit—her shoulders tight, her breath shallow, grief heavy as a stone. Chaos swirled around her. Vendors barked. Bells clanged. Dogs fought to be heard. Children darted between bodies. Even the smells overwhelmed—hot oil, crushed herbs, smoke. The world was noise, pressing from every side, threatening to claim her.

Then she remembered. In her coat pocket, tucked away like a secret, was the 3×5 card Pastor Jim had given her: *ONE IN CONSCIOUS UNITY WITH GOD CONSTITUTES A MAJORITY.* She didn't fully understand it, but when she pressed it to her chest, she felt steadied. Her breath lengthened. The chaos did not disappear, but it no longer commanded her.

That was when she noticed it. A narrow rusted gate between a fishmonger and a spice seller. The metal glowed faintly, like an ember that refused to die. Something in her—instinct, prayer, desperation—pulled her forward. She slipped through the gate unnoticed.

The air shifted. Jasmine drifted in the breeze. Birds stitched arcs between branches. A fountain whispered in the center of a hidden garden, and its sound invited her to lean closer, to listen with her whole life. For the first time since her father died, she exhaled completely. Tears came, but these were not hot and punishing. They were cool, gentle, like water flowing back into a dry riverbed.

On a weathered bench rested a parchment with her name written across it. The handwriting was steady, patient, strangely familiar. She opened it to find seven faint symbols glowing like constellations. One brightened as she touched it: *Peace.*

She sat with the word until it filled her. Peace was not silence—she had tried that. Peace was not escape—she had run before, only to find herself followed by the same pain. Peace was not pretending everything was fine—she had smiled until her cheeks ached, and it never held. Peace, she realized, was Presence. Spirit breathing through the noise. A treasure already within.

As she looked down, new words appeared on the parchment: **Trust—Peace grows where you release control.** She laughed softly. Control had been her armor since the funeral: flowers arranged, meals scheduled, paperwork organized, even her tears timed for midnight so no one could see. She had called it strength. But the fountain whispered otherwise—peace lived in release, not in holding everything together.

Another line formed: **Clarity—The lens that lets you see beyond the noise.** She thought of the cracked lens her father had left her, and how Holmes once said, *"Life is a mirror and will reflect back to the thinker what he thinks into it."* She pressed the card against her chest and felt warmth rise, as if her father's riddle had finally been solved: perception was the horizon of her life.

A third line glowed: **Surrender—The act that turns walls into gardens.** She remembered the rusted gate, how it had not been a barrier but an invitation. All her life she had believed the noise had the final word. But surrender was not defeat—it was finding a window already unlocked.

Then the garden shifted. Jesus stood by the fountain and touched the water until the ripples stilled. John sat beneath an olive tree, calm as dawn. "Peace isn't the world going quiet," Jesus said. "It is My life moving through your noise."

John added, "We were once on a boat, more afraid of the wind we could hear than the Presence we could not. He didn't remove the sea. Instead, He stilled us first."

Anna pressed the card tighter to her chest. Jesus said, "Breathe with Me. Peace is not escape. It is indwelling. Let Presence name, and then release, the sounds you fear."

Later that night, she told her brother Mark about the garden.

He grinned. "Figures. Dad never fixed the leaky faucet, but he left you a secret gate to Narnia." They laughed, and in that laughter grief loosened its grip. Emerson's voice returned: *"The invariable mark of wisdom is to see the miraculous in the common."* Humor was proof she was alive, a kind of holy light sneaking through.

But the parchment still glowed. When Anna touched the word Peace, it burned brighter. Six other symbols flickered in quiet promise. She whispered, "If peace has been here all along, what else have I missed?" The fountain rippled, and a voice, not loud but steady, answered: *"Keep walking. The map will show you."*

The next day she sat with Dr. Jim. Her brow was furrowed with questions. "How do I trust when life is so chaotic, when everything feels out of control? It's hard to believe Spirit is here when the world is this noisy."

He nodded gently. "Trust isn't certainty, Anna. It isn't control. It's surrendering the illusion you're alone. When we stop managing everything ourselves, we make space for Spirit to move. Trust is knowing the Presence is already here—steadying us, holding us, even in the storm."

She leaned closer. "What about clarity? How can I see through the noise when everything is so jumbled?"

"Clarity doesn't remove chaos," he said. "It tunes your inner lens. It lets you see what's real. It helps you hear Spirit whispering beneath the clamor, teaching you to tell the difference between what is fleeting and what is eternal."

Her shoulders softened. "And surrender?"

He smiled. "Surrender isn't giving up—it's letting go of the illusion of separateness. It's knowing Spirit is already working. Surrender is where walls become gardens. It's the sweetest act of trust: believing you are held, even when you cannot see how."

That night, Anna wrote in her journal. Words poured out in rhythm and breath until they became something else—something like poetry:

The Treasure of Peace
Noise everywhere.
Vendors shouting.
Bells clanging.
Grief gnawing.
I almost drowned in it—
till I pressed this truth to my chest:
One in unity with God is enough.
And the noise—
it softened.
Didn't vanish.
But it lost its grip.
Through the gate,
a hidden garden.
Stillness breathing.
Water whispering.
And I realized—
Peace isn't quiet.
Peace is Presence.
Peace is Spirit saying: *"I'm still here."*
The fountain rippled.
The map glowed.

And I heard it:
"Keep walking. There's more."

On Sunday, as the congregation lifted their voices, the refrain rose:

♪♪ *I Am... I said, the Presence is near, The power of Spirit is all that we hear. Every word spoken, in Love takes its stand, I Am is the doorway, to life's divine plan.* ♪♪

And Anna realized—peace was not the absence of noise. It was the Presence that carried her through it.

But as she folded the parchment that night, her eyes returned to the six symbols still waiting to be revealed. The next flickered like a lantern calling her forward.

The journey would continue.

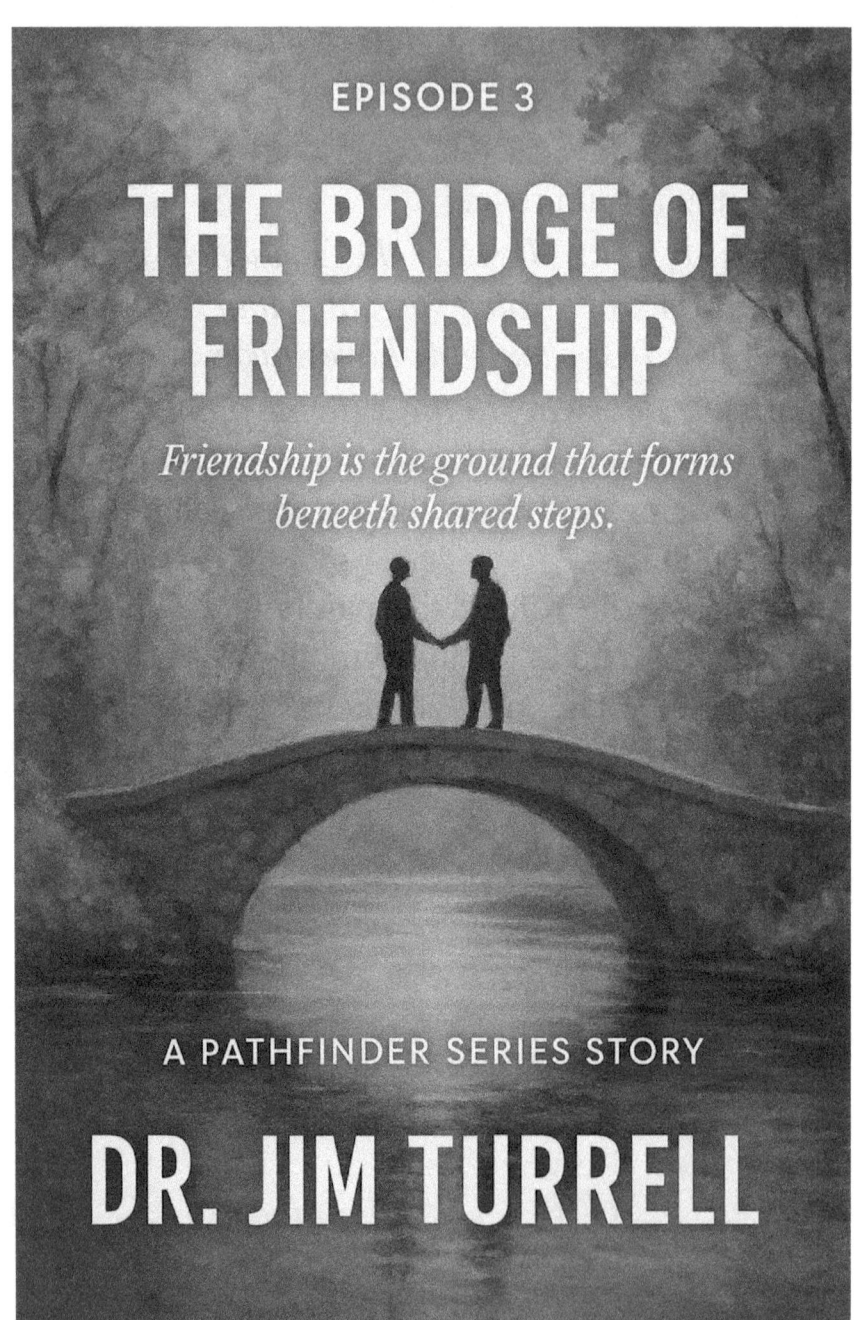

Episode 3
The Bridge of Friendship

Mark had always carried himself as the dutiful one. Where Anna questioned, he obeyed. Where Lila clung to control, he shouldered the burden. After their father's death, he believed his role was clear: hold the family together, bury his grief, and endure the silence like a soldier at his post.

But silence, he discovered, is heavier than grief itself.

Nights stretched long, stormy winds rattling the house, whispering his failures. He mistook duty for strength, but it hollowed him out. Emerson's words returned from his father's lessons: *"To be yourself in a world that is constantly trying to make you something else is the greatest accomplishment."* Mark thought being himself was selfish; he equated worth with responsibility. Thoreau's warning haunted him: *"Most men lead lives of quiet desperation and go to the grave with the song still in them."* And Anna's cracked lens only deepened the contrast—while she discovered perception, he still clung to performance.

Until one night, as the storm battered the roof, he whispered to himself: *"I can't do this alone."*

The next morning, weary and restless, he walked through town and reached the riverbank. That's when he saw it: a bridge forming out of mist—but only as long as he kept walking. Each step created planks beneath his feet, and when he stopped, the boards behind dissolved into vapor.

On the far side, Anna appeared. She carried her parchment with the glowing word *Peace*. As she stepped toward him, the bridge stretched. Mark moved too, and every shared step created the ground beneath them.

He laughed through sudden tears. *"So the bridge only exists when we walk it together?"*

Anna nodded. *"Friendship is the path God builds between souls."*

As they crossed, mist rose higher, and on the far bank Jesus stood with James and John.

James smiled, remembering. *"We learned to walk in pairs. He sent us two by two because storms are stubborn."*

Jesus looked at the planks forming under Mark and Anna's feet. *"Friendship is the ground love builds between souls. Where two or three gather in My name, I am there—as the strength between you."*

Mark felt the bridge grow steadier. For the first time, he realized his father never meant duty to be a prison; it was supposed to be connection.

Emerson's courage, Thoreau's honesty, Holmes' mirror—all of it began to make sense.

Jesus said, *"Keep walking together. Trust makes timber."*

That evening, Mark sat alone with his journal and remembered one of Thoreau's most famous lines from *Walden*:

*"I went to the woods because I wished to live deliberately,
to front only the essential facts of life,
and see if I could not learn what it had to teach,
and not, when I came to die,
discover that I had not lived."*

For years, Mark had mistaken duty for purpose. He thought his job was to carry, to endure, to keep the peace by holding silence. But Thoreau's words burned inside him: *live deliberately*. Life wasn't meant to be postponed or performed—it was meant to be lived fully, even at the risk of mistakes, even at the risk of loss.

He wrote: "I've lived as though life were a test I could fail, instead of a gift I could experience. I've hidden behind duty, but that's not living. Real life is stepping out, even trembling, into connection. Real life is risking myself for love, for friendship, for meaning."

And in that realization, he discovered something profound: the bridge of friendship is not just about walking together—it is about walking deliberately, choosing connection over isolation, authenticity over performance, love over duty.

The next Sunday, Anna sat with Dr. Jim and shared her brother's struggle.

"Mark thought duty was enough," she said softly. "But now he's learning it takes something more. Dr. Jim, is that… faith?"

Dr. Jim nodded. "Yes, Anna. Ernest Holmes said in *The Science of Mind* that *faith is the substance of things hoped for, the evidence of things not seen.* Faith is not blind belief. It's the inner knowing that the Spirit within us is greater than any storm around us."

"But Mark thought faith meant holding on tighter," Anna said. "That his worth came from responsibility."

"That's the confusion many of us carry," Dr. Jim replied. "Holmes also wrote in *This Thing Called You*: *'You are using the Law of Life every time you think. You can never get away from it.'* Faith isn't about clinging harder—it's about trusting that Spirit is already moving, already building the bridge beneath your feet as you walk."

Anna leaned closer. "So faith isn't about forcing outcomes?"

"No," Dr. Jim said. "Faith is letting go of the illusion of control and walking forward anyway. Holmes reminds us that *'faith is a mental attitude so inwardly embodied that the mind can no longer deny it.'* That's what Mark discovered. Duty without faith is heavy. But faith transforms duty into friendship, into love, into connection. Faith doesn't add weight—it lightens the load because it reminds us we are never walking alone."

Anna's eyes brightened. "So trust, clarity, surrender... they all grow out of faith."

"Exactly," Dr. Jim said. "Faith is the foundation that turns silence into song, burden into bridge, and fear into friendship."

Later that week, Mark told Lila what he had seen. She teased him: *"A magic bridge? Did Dad build it? If he did, better check the nails twice."* They all laughed, and laughter—once foreign—became oxygen again.

Yet the parchment still had more to say. As Mark and Anna crossed together, the mist lifted, and the bridge split in two directions—one glowing bright, the other shadowed.

Anna whispered, *"Which way do we go?"*

Mark held the map. Only one word flickered now: **Love.**

He picked up his pen and wrote a poem:

✏️ Slam Poem: The Bridge of Friendship

I thought I was drowning in silence—
till a bridge rose up from mist.
But here's the catch:
it only held
when another soul stepped beside me.
Friendship.
Not an accessory.
Not a bonus.
But the very wood God lays down
to keep us from the flood.
Connection.
Compassion.
Commitment.
That's the map.
Every step we take together
is a plank the storm cannot swallow.
And when I asked, *"Is this real?"*
the bridge itself replied:
"Only always."

The following Sunday, when Mark, Anna, Lila, and their mother Elena were in church, Dr. Jim had written a new refrain to be sung to his favorite song *Bridge Over Troubled Water.* Mark loved it so much that he hummed it all week:

I am your bridge when the waters rise,
Here in the storm, I will walk beside.

*Strong is the love that no flood can sever,
Friendship is Spirit, binding forever.*

Mark had learned that duty without love is a prison. But duty transformed by faith and friendship becomes a bridge. And as he and Anna stood where the bridge divided, the map revealed its next treasure: **Love.**

Thoreau's words whispered ahead, preparing them for what was to come: *"There is no remedy for love but to love more."*

✦ Reflection Questions for Your Journey

Duty vs. Connection: Where in your life have you mistaken duty for purpose? How might Spirit be inviting you to transform that duty into connection?

Faith's Real Meaning: Ernest Holmes says faith is "a mental attitude so inwardly embodied that the mind can no longer deny it." Where could you shift from clinging tighter to trusting deeper?

Living Deliberately: Thoreau went to the woods "to live deliberately." What is one step you can take this week to live more deliberately in your relationships, rather than drifting in silence or busyness?

Friendship as Bridge: Who in your life has God placed beside you, plank by plank, to help build the bridge of friendship? How can you honor that connection today?

Next Step: The map glows with one word—*Love.* What would it look like for you to walk toward that word with courage this week?

Episode 4
The Fire of Love

Anna and Mark crossed the bridge the way you cross a threshold you've been circling for years—slowly, aware that something on the other side will change you. Behind them, the creek argued with the stones in a silver whisper. Ahead, a small clearing opened, ringed by smooth, knee-high rocks.

In the center a fire burned that shouldn't have existed by any natural rule. It rose bright and steady, without smoke, without heat that scorched. What touched the flame wasn't destroyed—it was transformed.

There are fires that destroy and fires that reveal. This one was of the latter kind—the kind that doesn't take life but gives it back purified.

They stood without words, faces warmed by the soft glow.

Anna whispered, "Do you think this is what the map meant by Love?"

Mark nodded slowly. "If it is," he said, "what do we give it?"

Before either could move, the fire brightened. A voice rose—not through their ears, but through their bones:

Love grows when it's given.

Anna's breath caught. *Maybe peace doesn't come from the world,* she thought, *but from how the soul meets the world.*

Mark reached into his pocket and pulled out a folded letter—his resignation from a job that had drained his spirit. He had written it in courage but never sent it out of fear. Now he looked at the letter, then at the fire.

"Okay," he said quietly to no one and to God. "Okay."
He tossed the letter into the flames.

The paper didn't burn—it lifted, glowing, unfolding into a spray of black-ink music notes that fluttered upward like birds. They spiraled through the clearing and disappeared into the trees.

Mark let out a laugh that broke into tears. "It's giving me back my song," he said softly.

A thought stirred in him: *What if a man's duty isn't to hold his life together, but to let it unfold?* He realized that the safest thing he could ever do was to trust what was most alive within him.

Anna felt something shift inside. She reached into her tote, expecting pens and papers, but instead found what had come to define her life—**lists.** Lists of chores, calls, and plans she had written to keep herself safe from grief. Lists that had become her armor.

She fed the lists to the fire.

The words lifted off the page like flakes of bark, scattering as tiny white petals that drifted to the ground. Where they landed, green shoots pushed through the soil and bloomed into wildflowers.

Anna pressed a hand to her heart, half laughing, half crying.

"Love doesn't ask me to control," she said. "It asks me to give—and to live."

She suddenly remembered a truth she'd once read and dismissed as naïve: that *life simplifies itself when we trust it.* Now, watching her lists turn into blossoms, she finally understood—simplicity isn't about having less to do; it's about having more room for what matters.

The warmth of the fire deepened, and a sacred Presence filled the air—the same quiet grace they remembered from their father's bedtime blessings. They sat down on the circle of stones. The clearing seemed to hum, alive with peace.

Then the voice in the fire returned, calm and radiant:

Love is not consumed. Love consumes illusion.
When you give in love—time, forgiveness, kindness, courage—you do not lose.
You multiply. Giving is not subtraction; it's the fire that turns burden into blessing.

They didn't just hear it—they felt it. Around them, the flowers opened wider. The air seemed to breathe with them.

Mark thought about the old belief that love was fragile, that it could run out if not protected. But sitting there, he felt something different: love didn't need guarding—it was the Law that governed life itself. When it was given freely, it didn't fade; it flourished.

Anna pulled the map from her bag. Its parchment shimmered in the firelight. Across one corner, three glowing words appeared:

Generosity — Love multiplies when shared.

Transformation — Illusion burns; truth remains.

Courage — To give when fear whispers "hold back."

She read them aloud. Mark nodded, eyes still shining.

"Generosity," he said. "All my life I thought giving would empty me. But now I feel the opposite—the more I let go, the more alive I feel."

"Transformation," Anna said. "Maybe the fire doesn't burn the world around me—it burns away what's false inside me."

Mark smiled. "And courage—to give even when I'm afraid."

As the flames flickered, Anna realized that the map wasn't leading them somewhere new—it was leading them back to themselves.

They sat in silence until light itself felt sacred. Then they sensed a shift in the air—soft footsteps approaching.

Three figures emerged from the trees and stood beside the ring of stones: **Jesus, Mary Magdalene, and John.**

No grand entrance. Just presence—quiet, steady, holy.

Mary's eyes held compassion. "Love doesn't consume people," she said. "It burns away the lies about them."

John added gently, "He told us to love one another as He loved us. When we gave, we didn't lose. We became more ourselves."

Jesus looked at them both with fierce kindness. "Offer what you cling to," He said. "Watch Love turn chains into gifts."

Even heaven must repeat the truth, because humanity keeps confusing control with safety and fear with wisdom. Every time they release what they think protects them, they discover it was only what confined them.

Anna closed her eyes and found a hidden fear: the belief that she was only lovable when she was useful. She silently offered that belief to the flame. The fire shimmered, and in its place rose a quiet truth that filled her like breath: **You are loved because you are.**

She thought of how often she had looked outside for approval, when all along, love had been the quiet center of her being—unchangeable, constant, whole.

Mark stepped forward and offered his secret vow—the belief that if he stopped holding everything together, it would all fall apart. The fire answered with another truth: **You are held. You are part of a Wholeness that keeps everything together.**

He breathed out. It was as if he'd been carrying the weight of the universe only to learn the universe was carrying him.

They knelt without meaning to. The Presence around them felt like the heart of God itself. When they rose, the three figures had already faded back into the trees.

That evening, back home, they told their mother and sister everything.

Lila laughed, trying to hide the softening in her chest. "So you threw your to-do lists into a magic fire?"

Anna smiled. "Something like that."

Even Elena laughed, her eyes bright with memory. "I threw your father's hat away three times," she said, "and it kept coming back."

"Love resurrects ugly hats too," Mark said.

They all laughed, and the kitchen felt sacred—the kind of holiness that smells like soup and family.

Elena looked around at the glow of her children and thought, *Maybe heaven isn't a place after all—maybe it's the moment love takes over an ordinary room.*

As they quieted, the map on the table glowed again. This time two new words appeared: **Health** and **Joy.**

"The next chapters," Anna whispered.

The house gave a small shudder, as if it remembered something ancient. Shadows in the corners thickened—not with threat, but with meaning. Voices of doubt rose: *Who do you think you are? What if giving empties you? What if you've mistaken a fever for a flame?*

Anna touched the map. "If Love burns illusion, maybe these shadows show us what still needs to be offered."

Mark nodded. "Then we'll keep giving."

She felt a calm conviction rise within her: *The world doesn't test us; it reveals us.* The fire had shown her that truth burns gently, but it burns all the same.

The next day, Anna went to see Dr. Jim. Sunlight filled the sanctuary; candles flickered.

"Dr. Jim," she said, "the fire turned everything we gave it into something beautiful. But is that all love is—just letting go of what hurts?"

He smiled gently. "Love is a fire, yes—but it's not just for burning burdens. It's for transforming the self. Love asks us to surrender our need to control so the divine can move freely through us. When we give without attachment, Spirit multiplies the gift. Loss becomes gain. Chains become blossoms."

Anna thought about how the universe seems to echo back whatever you give it. *Maybe love isn't something we send out and hope returns—it's the very current that moves through everything when we stop resisting it.*

He leaned forward slightly. "Love isn't about forcing the harvest; it's about trusting the Life in the seed."

His words landed deep. She didn't feel certainty, but she felt willing. And that was enough.

That evening, Anna, Mark, Elena, and Lila returned to the clearing. The fire waited, patient as ever.

Lila stepped forward first. "I keep thinking if everything is measured, nothing will hurt," she said. "I'd like to hurt less."

She placed her ruler near the flames. The ruler warmed and turned into a soft ribbon of music that drifted through the trees—its need to measure giving way to the rhythm of love itself.

Elena brought her silence—the quiet she had wrapped around herself since her husband's passing. She laid it by the fire. It lifted like a veil and settled again as gentle openness, a space where laughter and tears could rest together.

Mark placed an old key by the fire. "For all the doors I guard that are already unlocked," he said. The key melted and became a tiny green sprout. The lock had always been a seed.

Anna stepped forward last. "Take the part of me that believes I'm only worthy when I'm needed," she whispered.

The fire moved like breath, like prayer. A soft knowing filled her heart: **You are loved—and that is enough.**

They stood together as night gathered its stars. None of them felt emptied—only lighter, freer, more alive.

In the days that followed, love showed itself in small ways:

Mark fixed Mr. Lopez's porch light, not out of duty but out of joy.

Lila hosted dinner and didn't rush to clean. Elena let herself receive kindness without apologizing.

Anna returned a difficult call, not with advice, but with presence.

Whenever fear whispered *hold back*, they remembered the fire and the way love had given everything back, transformed.

Love doesn't remove the ordinary—it sanctifies it. The porch light, the phone call, the messy living room—all become altars where giving turns into grace.

That night Anna dreamed of the map again. Two new lands glowed at its edge: **Health** and **Joy**. Between them, the hills shimmered with shadowy shapes—doubts waiting to be burned into light.

When she woke, the map on the table pulsed with the same words. She knocked on Mark's door. He stood there, guitar in hand, hair wild with morning music.

"Health and Joy," she said.

He smiled. "Then we keep giving." She smiled back. "Then we keep giving."

They returned to the clearing at dawn. The fire was low but alive. Together they offered what still held them back—old vows, small fears, and the stories that said joy had to be earned. Each offering rose, then returned as gratitude, as play, as freedom.

Anna stood tall, feeling at home in her own spirit. Then she spoke these words:

Slam Poem: The Fire of Love
A fire that burns,
but nothing turns to ash.
I fed it my fears—
they came back as flowers.
I fed it my chains—
they came back as wings.
Love does not shrink when given.
Love expands.
Love is the math of heaven:
Give everything,
and find yourself multiplied.
And the fire whispered:
**"Stop guarding your gifts.
Throw them in.
Watch what happens when love burns illusions."**

They stood in a silence that felt like bread breaking. The clearing breathed with them. On the walk home, Mark began to hum. Anna joined him. Lila laughed and missed a note, and no one cared. Elena's eyes shone with joy too wide to hide.

At the threshold of their home, Anna turned back toward the bridge and whispered a new refrain—one the fire had left in her heart:

Closing Refrain — All You Need Is Love (Adapted)

> All you need is Love—
> the fire that never dies.
> All you need is Love—
> it gives and multiplies.
> Love is the doorway
> where Spirit sets us free.
> All you need is Love,
> and Love lives in thee.

✸ **Love is the fire that strips away illusion and multiplies when given.**

Here are **five reflective discussion questions** crafted for *Episode 4: The Fire of Love*. Each question invites readers (or a congregation) to pause, contemplate, and connect the story's metaphysical insights with their own spiritual experience.

1. The Nature of Transformation

When Mark's resignation letter becomes music and Anna's lists bloom into flowers, the story shows that true transformation doesn't destroy—it reveals.

What in your own life might need to pass through Love's fire—not to be lost, but to be made new?

2. The Illusion of Control

Anna realizes that "Love doesn't ask me to control—it asks me to give and to live." **Where in your life are you trying to manage** what really needs to be trusted? How might letting go create more peace, not less?

3. The Courage to Surrender

The fire teaches that "giving is not subtraction; it's the fire that turns burden into blessing."

What fear keeps you from giving fully—of time, forgiveness, or yourself—and what might happen if you released that fear into Love's flame?

4. The Law of Multiplication

When each character gives something away, they receive something greater in return. **How does this story challenge the belief that giving depletes us? Where have you experienced generosity or kindness multiplying rather than diminishing your spirit?**

5. The Practice of Love in the Ordinary

By the story's end, love shows itself not through miracles but through small, human acts—fixing a porch light, sharing a meal, making a call. **How might you turn an ordinary moment this week into an altar for love? What small action could become your own offering to the fire?**

THE PATHFINDER SERIES

EPISODE 5

THE CROWN OF HEALTH

Health is harmony of
body, mind, and Spirit.

DR. JIM TURRELL

Episode 5
The Crown of Health

The morning after the Fire of Love had faded into ember-light, the forest breathed as if it too were at peace. Mist curled through the branches like incense rising from an unseen altar. Anna, Mark, Lila, and Elena stood in the clearing where the eternal flame had burned. The ground still shimmered faintly with warmth, as though the earth remembered what it had witnessed.

Anna knelt near the ashes, tracing a small circle in the dirt. "It's strange," she whispered. "The fire's gone, but I still feel it in me."

Dr. Jim smiled, resting a hand on his walking staff. "That's how true love works. It doesn't stay in the wood—it moves into the heart."

They had learned that love multiplies when given, that it refines rather than consumes. But something new stirred now, something unfinished. The map, tucked in Anna's satchel, began to hum faintly—like a heartbeat calling them forward. Lila noticed first. "It's glowing again."

Mark sighed but smiled. "Of course it is. One fire dies, another begins."

Elena adjusted her shawl. "Let's see where Spirit leads us next."

The map shimmered open, casting a golden glow across their faces. Letters appeared slowly in the air above it, pulsing with life: **Stewardship.**

They set out the next morning along a narrow mountain trail. The air grew thin and bright, and silence surrounded them except for the rhythmic crunch of their footsteps. By dusk, they reached a spring that poured from a cleft in the rocks. The water was so clear it seemed invisible until it rippled.

As they sat around their small fire that night, Anna broke the quiet. "Dr. Jim," she said, "that story you told—the old man who said we're stewards of life, not owners—keeps stirring in me. We live as if life were a treasure chest with a lock. But what if it's not limited at all? What if it's eternal, infinite?"

Dr. Jim smiled, his eyes reflecting the flames. "Exactly, Anna. Life isn't a possession—it's a gift entrusted to us. Fear makes us clutch at it, as if it might run out. But life is Spirit's river, always flowing, asking us not to hoard, but to tend, to share, to steward."

He reached down, scooped a handful of water, and let it pour through his fingers. "See this? The spring doesn't worry it will run dry—it simply flows because that is its nature. Spirit is the same."

Mark leaned closer to the fire. "So stewardship isn't about control?"

Dr. Jim shook his head. "Not control—trust. Care. Reverence. We're caretakers of what God gives, not gatekeepers of what we think we own."

Elena smiled gently. "Your father used to say, 'You don't keep the light—you pass it along.'"

Dr. Jim nodded. "Emerson said, 'The creation of a thousand forests is in one acorn.' That's stewardship. One life, faithfully tended, can multiply beyond measure."

Anna's brow softened. "So the more I care for life, the more life grows through me?"

"Exactly. Thoreau said, 'Only that day dawns to which we are awake.' Stewardship begins with awakening—to what's already here, already entrusted to your hands."

Mark considered that, then said, "And Holmes said something about the mirror, didn't he?"

"Yes. 'Life is a mirror and will reflect back to the thinker what he thinks into it.' Stewardship begins in thought. You don't just tend the world—you tend your own mind first."

A spark leapt from the fire and rose into the night. Anna followed it with her eyes. "So the spark isn't gone—it's just part of the sky now."

Dr. Jim smiled. "Exactly. Stewardship is the art of trusting the eternal flow already moving through you."

By morning, they followed the trail down into a valley that opened into a vast meadow shimmering with dew. Sunlight spilled over the grass like gold dust, and the sound of birds wove through the wind like a hymn. Anna stretched her arms wide, drinking in the beauty.

"So much of the world lives in survival mode," she said. "Afraid of losing what it thinks is scarce. But if life is infinite, then our calling isn't survival—it's harmony."

Dr. Jim grinned. "Yes. To be a steward is to tune your body, mind, and spirit into the harmony of the Infinite. It's not about force—it's about alignment. When you trust life's rhythm, you stop rowing upstream with fear and start gliding with love."

They came to a small cottage at the edge of the meadow. The door was open, and inside sat a wooden table laid with fruit, bread, and a golden crown resting on a pillow.

Mark raised an eyebrow. "Another crown?"

Dr. Jim stepped closer and read the engraving around its rim: *The Crown of Stewardship—For those who live in harmony with the Whole.*

They gathered around the table as the crown began to glow softly. When Lila reached out and touched it, an image appeared—rivers, trees, mountains, and stars, all flowing in rhythm like a living symphony.

Dr. Jim spoke softly. "Thoreau said, 'Our life is frittered away by detail… simplify, simplify.' True health is found in simplicity—rest, nourishment, honest thought."

Anna looked down at her hands. "I've spent my life trying to organize everything—control things. Maybe that's not stewardship at all. Maybe it's noise."

Dr. Jim nodded. "The steward's task is to listen for balance. Holmes wrote, 'We should be careful to think only those thoughts we want to experience.' Guard your thoughts the way you guard your home. Let in only what brings peace."

Elena's eyes glistened as she looked at the crown. "And Emerson said, 'The first wealth is health.' Harmony is wealth—it's the abundance of life in balance, cared for with reverence."

They each touched the crown. Anna felt her heart slow to match her breath. Mark heard a hum deep inside him, like the earth singing. Lila felt her restlessness melt into calm. And Elena felt her heart open until tears filled her eyes—tears not of sorrow, but gratitude.

Dr. Jim smiled. "You see? Life plays through us like music. When you live in balance, you don't force the melody—you become it."

That night, they camped in the meadow beneath a velvet sky. The wind stirred softly through the grass. Anna gazed into the fire. "Dr.

Jim… what about the chaos and hate in the world? It feels so opposite of all this harmony."

Dr. Jim watched the flames dance. "Chaos is real, but not eternal. It's only ripples on the sea of life. Our work as stewards is renewal—to return, again and again, to trust, to love, to care. Stewardship isn't perfection. It's beginning again with every dawn."

Mark nodded. "Like starting over each day."

"Yes. Holmes said, 'When we learn to trust the universe, we shall be happy, prosperous, and well.' Renewal begins with trust."

Lila smiled faintly. "Thoreau said, 'Every morning was a cheerful invitation to make my life of equal simplicity and innocence with Nature itself.' Every sunrise is a second chance."

Elena added softly, "And Emerson said, 'What lies behind us and what lies before us are tiny matters compared to what lies within us.' Renewal flows from within. It never runs dry."

Anna looked up at the stars. "So to steward life is to trust that every moment is a beginning?"

"Yes," said Dr. Jim. "Renewal is your birthright. Care is your calling. Love is the rhythm that never ends."

Silence followed—long and deep. Then Anna noticed something wondrous. The crown was glowing again, brighter than before. Its light poured outward, not as fire, but as warmth that seemed to bless everything around them. And then, faintly, they heard music—not from any instrument, but from the world itself. The whisper of wind, the rustle of grass, even the beating of their own hearts joined in one living song.

Mark broke the stillness first. He picked up the crown and set it on his head. "Great," he groaned. "Now I feel guilty about all the donuts I've ever eaten."

Lila burst into laughter. "Don't worry, the crown doesn't judge. It just reminds you to choose apples more often."

Anna grinned. "Or at least balance the donuts with a jog."

Elena chuckled, her laughter like wind chimes. "Maybe the crown should come with a side of laughter."

Dr. Jim laughed too. "It does. "Sometimes the most spiritual thing you can do is laugh." ("Sometimes the most spiritual thing you can do is laugh. Joy is part of ...") It keeps the soul light."

Their laughter rolled across the meadow until tears ran down their cheeks. Even the crown seemed to pulse with joy. They realized that laughter, too, was a form of stewardship—the care of the spirit through delight.

When dawn came, they packed their things and prepared to move on. The crown rested on the map, glowing steadily. Then, without warning, the parchment unfolded itself, revealing two treasures shining at once—**Joy** and **Prosperity.**

Two paths appeared before them: one leading to a great hall filled with music and laughter, the other to a vast garden overflowing with fruit and light.

Anna turned to the others. "Do we choose Joy or Prosperity?"

The crown shimmered, and a voice—clear, gentle, and unmistakable—spoke within each of their hearts. "One reveals the other."

The air grew still. Even the birds seemed to pause.

Dr. Jim closed his eyes, smiling. "Then we follow where love leads."

They stood hand in hand, facing the twin paths of radiance. Between them glowed the golden light of trust, care, and reverence—the living essence of stewardship. And as they took their first step forward, the crown's voice whispered again, softer this time but full of promise: "Stewardship is the art of love made visible."

Later that evening, when they stopped beside a small pond, Anna wandered to the water's edge. Moonlight rippled across its surface like liquid glass. Something small gleamed in the mud near her boot. She knelt and lifted it carefully—a single acorn.

She turned it over in her palm and remembered Emerson's words: *"The creation of a thousand forests is in one acorn."*

She smiled, her heart swelling with quiet awe. The crown of stewardship, she realized, wasn't just an object of gold—it was the awareness that every act of care plants a seed for others to grow beneath.

Behind her, Mark was setting up camp. Lila hummed softly as she spread the blankets, and Elena tended the fire. The glow from their little circle of light reflected in the water, merging with the moon.

Anna looked at the acorn again. "Thank you, Life," she whispered, "for trusting me to tend your garden."

The wind carried her words away—not as sound, but as blessing. Somewhere beyond the next hill, the treasures of Joy and Prosperity waited, glowing softly in the promise of dawn.

And the night, tender and alive, wrapped them in silence, as though the whole universe whispered back, *You are the steward of my love.*

And, as Anna sighed she caught Dr. Jim's attention and added a poetic statement framed as if Dr. Jim said it:

> A fire that burns,
> but nothing turns to ash.
> I fed it my fears —

they came back as flowers.
I fed it my chains —
they came back as wings.
I fed it my pain —
it rose as song.
Love does not shrink when given.
Love expands.
Love is the math of heaven:
Give everything and find yourself multiplied.
The flame whispered:
"Stop guarding your gifts.
Throw them in.
Watch what happens
when love burns illusions."
And I did.
What returned was health —
not just of body, but of soul.
Love is the crown,
and joy is its jewel.

The last line lingered in the air like incense. Anna's eyes glowed with understanding.

"So, health isn't something we chase — it's something we awaken to?"

Dr. Jim smiled "Exactly. Love restores what fear divides. And joy — joy is the laughter of God echoing through a healed heart."

Next: "The Feast of Joy" — where laughter becomes prayer, and gratitude becomes prosperity.

Lesson 5 — The Crown of Health: Wholeness as the Natural State of Spirit

What does "health" mean beyond the physical body?

How might true health include harmony of mind, emotion, and spirit—and what practices help you nurture that wholeness?

In what ways do your thoughts and beliefs shape the experience of your body?

Reflect on Ernest Holmes' idea that *"Life is a mirror and will reflect back to the thinker what he thinks into it."* How might this guide your healing process?

How can you become a loving steward of your own well-being?

What daily choices—small or large—could express greater reverence for the sacred gift of your life?

Where do you notice imbalance, and how might Spirit be inviting you toward alignment?

Consider Thoreau's wisdom: *"Our life is frittered away by detail… simplify, simplify."* What would simplicity look like for your body and soul right now?

How might gratitude and joy function as medicine?

When have laughter, appreciation, or beauty brought renewal to your heart or healing to your body?

Episode 6
The Feast of Joy

The path ahead of them glowed as though it remembered every footstep that had ever walked it. The air shimmered with that peculiar stillness that only occurs when something sacred is about to happen. Anna walked between her brother Mark and her sister Lila, carrying the crown of health they had found in the previous clearing. The gold of it reflected the unseen light around them, flickering with the pulse of their own hearts.

They followed the luminous road until it curved toward a grand wooden door that looked older than time. Its surface was carved with patterns of vines and stars, and above its arch were three simple letters: **A · S · K.**

Mark chuckled softly, trying to mask his awe. "Guess they really meant it," he said.

Anna traced the letters with her fingers. The carvings felt alive, humming faintly beneath her touch. "Ask," she whispered, "Seek... Knock." The syllables hung in the air like keys waiting to fit their locks.

She knocked once, gently, and the door responded as if it had been waiting centuries for that sound. It opened with a deep sigh, releasing a current of warm air scented with bread, fruit, and wine.

They stepped through.

The hall that opened before them was vast beyond comprehension, yet welcoming — the way a sunrise feels before it fully arrives. Long tables stretched from horizon to horizon, each one overflowing with food that shimmered in the soft golden light: baskets of figs and loaves, pitchers of clear water that caught the rainbow, goblets filled with laughter disguised as wine. Music rippled through the space — not from instruments, but from the joyful murmur of human voices, of clinking glasses, of gratitude spoken like prayer.

At the far end of the hall, high above the tables, a great banner swayed gently in an unseen breeze. It read:

JOY IS A FEAST. SHARE IT.

Anna stopped in wonder. "Is this… for us?" she asked a passing steward, a kindly man with eyes that reflected galaxies.

The steward smiled. "Not for you," he said. "For *all*. Joy is never private. It is given, and it multiplies."

As they moved among the tables, they noticed a strange and beautiful pattern: the food on their plates appeared only after they had first served someone else. If they tried to fill their own plates first, nothing came. But when they offered bread or poured a cup for another, their own cups filled again, richer than before.

Lila burst out laughing. "So the math of joy," she exclaimed, "is generosity squared!"

Mark grinned. "Now that's a gospel even I can calculate."

The steward nodded approvingly. "Exactly. In this hall, to give is to receive. Joy exists only in circulation. What you pass on becomes your portion."

Anna felt tears rise unbidden. "It's like the world we were meant to live in," she whispered. "No lack, no fear, no guarding — just giving."

They sat together, hands brushing over shared plates, hearts softening into gratitude. The hall seemed to breathe with them, expanding each time they laughed, glowing brighter with every kind gesture.

Then, from across the hall, came a familiar sound — laughter that carried a rhythm older than memory. They turned toward it and saw a long table where a small circle of men were gathered. Among them was a figure radiant yet ordinary, wearing the simple robe of a traveler. Jesus sat at the center, eyes alight with mirth. He broke bread with a grin and passed the basket down the line. Andrew and Philip were beside him, shaking their heads in astonished delight as the baskets, though passed again and again, never emptied.

"Ask," Jesus said, his voice like wind through olive leaves. "Ask and let Heaven's generosity move through you. Seek, and notice joy already set like a table before you. Knock, and the doorway opens into the feast of life. Joy multiplies in the passing."

Andrew whispered to Philip, "Remember Cana, when the water became wine and joy filled a wedding that had almost ended? And on the hillside, when bread and fish multiplied until everyone was fed? Whether it was wine for a few or bread for thousands, joy always spread."

Lila passed a plate toward an old woman beside her, and immediately her own plate filled again. The message was clear: joy doesn't run out — it runs over.

Mark reached for another slice of bread, grinning, but as soon as his fingers touched it, the bread vanished. "Hey!" he said. "My bread just disappeared!"

Anna smirked. "Did you pass it first?"

He sighed, laughing. "So even the bread is preaching stewardship now?"

Their laughter rang like bells. The whole hall seemed to join in, rippling with mirth that healed more than it entertained. In that laughter was freedom — the kind that only comes when you finally realize you were never meant to be in charge of abundance, only to participate in it.

As the laughter subsided, a deep chord sounded from somewhere unseen — not quite music, not quite thunder — and the light shifted. At the far end of the hall, a great door of shining gold began to open, slowly, as if waiting for the right moment to reveal what lay beyond. Through its widening crack spilled the light of morning — not sunlight, but something purer, more alive. They glimpsed a garden filled with radiance, trees heavy with fruit, rivers running like liquid crystal. Prosperity itself seemed to hum there, shimmering like dawn made visible.

Anna leaned forward, eyes wide. "Is that what's next?" she whispered.

The steward nodded. "Yes," he said. "But only those who know their worth can enter. Abundance cannot be seen by eyes that believe they are undeserving."

A silence fell, full of thought. The truth landed gently but deeply. Each of them felt its echo: joy and abundance are not earned by effort — they are revealed by worthiness.

Later, as the music softened, Anna sat apart for a while, her plate untouched, her gaze resting on the feast before her. Dr. Jim came to sit beside her, the lamplight catching a warmth in his eyes that felt like both teacher and friend.

"I've been thinking," Anna said softly. "Life feels like this hall — an endless banquet. But most of us live as if it's a famine. We act like we have to grab what we can before it's gone. We hoard, we protect, we compete — as though the table might be cleared without warning. But what if that's all a lie? What if life itself is this feast — infinite, overflowing, waiting for us to trust it?"

Dr. Jim smiled, the corners of his mouth turning upward as if he'd been waiting for her to say those exact words. "That," he said, "is the awakening. The divine truth is that life — whole, everlasting, and limitless — is always offering itself. There's never a lack in Spirit, only a lack of awareness. Humanity forgets this because it listens to fear more than to truth — the fear of not enough, of not being enough, of time running out. But when we awaken to the divine rhythm, we see what was always there: life is a continual giving. The banquet is already set."

Anna nodded slowly. "Then joy isn't something I have to earn or find — it's what happens when I stop resisting life's generosity."

"Exactly," said Dr. Jim. "To ask is to open. To seek is to perceive. To knock is to act in faith. These are not commands from a distant God — they are invitations from the Spirit within you. Every time you ask, you expand the vessel. Every time you seek, you deepen the awareness. Every time you knock, you prove your trust. And that trust is what opens the door to abundance."

He leaned closer, his voice low but radiant. "You see, joy isn't the reward for good living — it's the natural fragrance of the soul when it's aligned with divine flow. When we give freely, we don't lose; we participate in circulation. When we love, we don't spend; we multiply. It's divine mathematics. The universe is built on generosity, not scarcity."

Anna looked at the hall around them — every table filled, every person laughing, every exchange of food and kindness making the light brighter. "Then everything we give — love, forgiveness, kindness — it multiplies?"

"Yes," said Dr. Jim. "It doesn't leave you poorer; it proves you're part of something infinite. Think of the sun. Does it grow dim because it shines? Or the ocean — does it shrink because it gives of itself to the clouds? No. The source remains full. So it is with you. The more you give from your fullness, the more you reveal the truth that there was never any lack. You are not giving something away; you are giving something *through*."

Anna felt a stillness bloom inside her chest, the kind that feels like understanding without words. "So... life isn't about acquiring, is it? It's about remembering we already have."

Dr. Jim's eyes softened with affection. "You are a steward of infinite life," he said. "You were never meant to hold it, only to let it flow. Every time you share, you affirm your connection to the Source. Every time you release, you discover you are replenished. When we finally trust that, fear dissolves — because fear is only the shadow cast by the belief in limitation. Gratitude becomes the natural language of the soul that knows it is safe in an infinite universe."

Mark and Lila joined them, still glowing from laughter. Mark, ever the practical one, said, "You know, I used to think joy was the *result* of things going right — good health, enough money, people liking you. But I'm starting to see that joy comes *first,* and then the rest follows."

Dr. Jim smiled. "That's the reversal that changes everything. Joy is not the effect — it's the cause. It's the consciousness that precedes abundance. When you live joyfully, you magnetize everything needed for that joy to continue."

Lila clapped her hands. "So that's why the food keeps appearing! It's like joy creates the supply!"

Anna laughed, the sound bright and clean. "The more we share, the more the hall expands."

"The hall," Dr. Jim said, "is your own soul. Each act of generosity expands its walls. Each grateful breath fills it with more light. And when your inner hall grows large enough, the outer world begins to reflect it."

The music rose again, soft but jubilant. Across the room, people were standing, raising cups, embracing. The feast was no longer just a meal; it had become a living symphony of connection. Every smile seemed to feed another, every word of kindness stirred the air like incense.

At the head table, Jesus lifted his cup high. "Joy," he said, "is the taste of God remembered."

The words rippled through the hall, and for a moment, time itself seemed to bow in reverence.

Anna closed her eyes and breathed deeply. She saw in her mind not just this hall, but the entire world — cities, oceans, mountains — all as one vast table of divine provision. Every act of love another plate passed, every forgiveness another cup filled.

Then she felt something else — a whisper, almost like a thought not her own: *The feast has never ended. Humanity has simply forgotten to sit down.*

Her eyes opened again. The hall seemed even brighter now, every face radiant with shared light. She reached for her cup and lifted it toward her companions. "To the feast," she said.

"To joy that multiplies," Mark replied.

They drank, and laughter rose again, blending with the unseen music that held the whole hall together. The air shimmered, and somewhere far off, the golden door to the next garden stood waiting.

As they prepared to rise, the steward returned. "Before you go," he said, "remember this: ask, seek, and knock are not commands of need but of trust. They are the rhythm of a soul in harmony with its Source. Ask — and you remember that life listens. Seek — and you remember that truth is everywhere. Knock — and you remember that the door has always been open."

Then he bowed and disappeared into the brightness.

Anna turned to her companions, her eyes shining with new understanding. "Maybe the miracle isn't that the bread never runs out," she said. "Maybe it's that love never does."

Dr. Jim smiled. "Exactly. The bread is just love made visible. And that," he said, rising with them, "is the Feast of Joy."

The hall began to dissolve into light. The tables melted into golden streams, the laughter into song, until all that remained was radiance and the faint echo of the words written above the first door: **A · S · K.**

Ask — and you will remember the abundance within.
Seek — and you will discover joy hiding in plain sight.

Knock — and you will enter the life that never ends.

The light faded into silence. Somewhere beyond, a garden awaited, blooming with the next mystery. Anna could not rest until she wrote a poem that expressed her understanding of what her heart revealed.

Slam Poem: "The Feast of Joy"
I asked—
and the door unlocked.
I sought—
and the table stretched long.
I knocked—
and the hall itself answered:
"Sit. Share. Laugh. Live."
Joy is not dessert.
Joy is the feast.
The more you pass it on,
the more it fills your plate.
And the hall whispered:
"Joy never runs out—
it runs over."

Closing Refrain — Adapted from *Ode to Joy*

Joyful, joyful, Spirit shining,
Hearts awake, Your love we sing.
Ask and doors of grace swing open,

> Seek and find Your everything.
> Knock, and every feast is ready,
> Joy abounds, it multiplies.
> Sharing love, the hall resounding,
> God's own presence never dies.

Philosophical Meaning:

Joy is the revelation of divine sufficiency. It is the realization that life's true nature is overflow. Asking, seeking, and knocking are not actions of desperation but gestures of faith — the soul remembering its source. In this realization, scarcity is unmasked as illusion, and generosity becomes the natural order. Joy, like light, increases only by being shared. It is not a possession but a participation in the eternal circulation of Spirit.

Joy is the feast that multiplies when it's shared — and ASK is the doorway in.

Reflective Self-Inquiry — "The Feast Within"

When I imagine life as an endless banquet, where in me still believes the table will run out? What fear, habit, or belief still tells me I must guard, compete, or earn what Spirit freely gives?

How do I "feed others first" in my daily life — and where do I still hold back? Can I see that my giving (of time, compassion, forgiveness) is not depletion but divine multiplication?

When have I mistaken asking for begging, or seeking for striving?

How might I approach "Ask, Seek, Knock" as a posture of trust instead of effort — an invitation to flow, not force?

What does generosity look like in my inner world?

Can I offer the same open-handed kindness to myself that I offer to others — recognizing that I, too, am part of the feast?

What would my life look like if I truly believed that joy never runs out?

What choices, relationships, or creative acts would flow naturally if I lived as a joyful steward of infinite supply?

Episode 7

THE KINGDOM OF PROSPERITY

This episode reveals that prosperity is not what we keep, but what flows through us.

A Pathfinder Series Story
Dr. Jim Turrell

Episode 7
The Kingdom of Prosperity

The path had grown quieter as they walked, yet something in the silence felt vast and alive. It wasn't emptiness — it was invitation. The forest around them seemed to breathe with them, the wind moving through the branches like a slow exhale of the Divine. The glow from the map — their faithful guide through every mystery — now pulsed like a living heartbeat in Anna's hand.

They had crossed bridges and fires, found crowns and feasts, faced both illusion and illumination. Each step had stripped something away, revealing a greater truth underneath. Now, as dawn began to stir the horizon, they came to the final gate.

It stood at the edge of the valley — taller than the trees, older than memory. Its surface shimmered with carvings of vines heavy with fruit, and across its arch glowed the words:

"Where your treasure is, there your heart will be also."

The air was different here — rich and still, as though all of heaven had gathered in to listen.

Anna's voice came softly. "This must be the final treasure."

Mark nodded. "Feels like the world is holding its breath."

Lila stepped closer, brushing her fingertips against the carved vines. "It's beautiful… but it's closed."

Dr. Jim joined them, his expression calm, luminous. "The Kingdom of Prosperity doesn't open by key," he said. "It opens by offering."

They looked down. Before the gate were four smooth stones, each engraved with a single word:

Time. Talent. Treasure. Trust.

The message was clear — they were being asked to give something of themselves.

Anna reached first. From her satchel, she pulled the folded lists she once lived by — plans, schedules, rules that had become her illusion of safety. "These lists were how I tried to control my life," she said quietly. "But control is not care. I lay down my time — not as something to manage, but as something to share."

She placed the papers upon the stone marked *Time.*

Mark knelt next. He pulled from his pocket his guitar pick, worn smooth from years of avoidance as much as use. "My music was always my hiding place," he said, his voice trembling slightly. "But it was never meant to hide me — it was meant to heal. I give my talent to Spirit, to serve, not to prove."

He placed it gently on the stone marked *Talent.*

Lila stepped forward, holding a small silver coin. "It's not much," she said, smiling softly. "But it's what I have. I give it with gratitude, not fear. My treasure is my trust."

Elena came last. Around her neck hung the pendant her husband had given her long ago — a small locket containing a faded photograph. She held it a moment longer, eyes glistening. "I give my grief," she whispered. "It has been my burden and my teacher. But now I give it back to love."

She placed it upon the stone marked *Trust.*

For a heartbeat, nothing happened. Then, from the heart of the gate, a light began to spread — gentle, golden, alive. The carved vines rippled as if breathing, their fruit bursting into radiant bloom. The air filled with fragrance — citrus, cedar, and sunlight all at once.

The gate opened.

They stepped through together.

What met them on the other side was not a temple or a throne, but a garden unlike anything they had ever seen. It pulsed with life — a landscape of rivers, meadows, and orchards, every leaf shimmering as though lit from within.

The grass sang softly underfoot. The rivers laughed. The very air carried the vibration of gratitude. It wasn't a place you entered; it was a consciousness you remembered.

Jesus stood beside a stream that ran like liquid crystal, smiling as though greeting old friends. Peter and Matthew sat nearby, their faces aglow in the gentle light.

"Welcome," Jesus said, spreading his hands. "You've come far, but the Kingdom was never distance — it was recognition. You did not arrive here. You awakened here."

Peter laughed, rubbing his calloused palms together. "You know, I once gave up a boat and thought I was losing everything. Turned out I was trading nets for miracles."

Matthew nodded. "And I left my ledgers thinking I was walking away from security. Now I see that what I gave up was chains. Prosperity isn't what you hold — it's what flows."

Jesus turned toward the gate where their offerings still shimmered faintly. "Lay down what you fear to lose," he said. "The Kingdom opens where love circulates. Life was never about holding — it was about allowing."

The family listened, hearts full, the truth sinking deeper with every breath.

Later, as evening gold touched the garden, Anna sat beside Dr. Jim beneath a tree so radiant its bark seemed woven from light. The air smelled faintly of rain and roses.

"Dr. Jim," she said softly, "I keep thinking about how much I used to chase — time, success, approval. It was like I believed if I stopped striving, everything would fall apart. But now I see… it's when I stop grasping that life begins to flow."

Dr. Jim smiled gently. "That's the paradox of divine prosperity, Anna. You can't store what was made to circulate. Life isn't a bank account — it's a river. The more freely you give, the more freely it moves through you. When you give your time, you plant presence in another's life. When you give your talent, you become a conduit for Spirit's creativity. When you give your treasure, you declare your trust in an infinite Source. True prosperity isn't accumulation — it's alignment."

Anna nodded slowly, her eyes reflecting the garden's light. "So prosperity isn't something I earn — it's something I express."

"Exactly," said Dr. Jim. "It's not about what you keep. It's about what you release with faith. Emerson said, *'The measure of mental health is the disposition to find good everywhere.'* The same is true of prosperity — it's not about how much you have, but how much good you see and share."

He leaned on his staff, the wood catching a golden gleam. "Holmes called it *the circulation of life*. When we understand that giving and receiving are one act — two sides of divine law — fear dissolves. There is no 'outflow' and 'inflow.' There is only the movement of love through an open heart."

Anna smiled, her tears falling freely now. "Then everything I've given... it was never gone."

"No," said Dr. Jim. "It became you."

As twilight deepened, the others joined them by a small pond at the garden's center. The surface mirrored the stars beginning to bloom overhead.

Mark watched the reflection of his guitar pick gleaming faintly beneath the water. "It's funny," he said. "I gave my music away, and now I hear it everywhere — in the wind, in the water, in the laughter."

Lila laughed gently. "Spirit's greatest remix."

Even Elena smiled. "Your father used to say that joy is just love with wings."

Dr. Jim chuckled. "And Thoreau said, *'Wealth is the ability to fully experience life.'* That's what prosperity really is — the capacity to say yes to life, even in uncertainty, even in change."

They sat quietly for a long time, the night alive with the hum of unseen life. Then, in the distance, the sound of laughter drifted across the meadow — familiar and bright. They turned and saw a gathering near the gate — the friends and faces they had met throughout their journey: the rabbi by the fire, the artist by the bridge, the steward from the feast. All were there, carrying candles, their light rippling like a tide of remembrance.

Each stepped forward, placing their own gifts beside the stones — a painter's brush, a loaf of bread, a small child's drawing, a musician's bow. Every gift seemed to dissolve into the earth, then reappear as blossoms across the field.

Anna whispered, "So everyone's part of this... everyone's offering keeps the Kingdom alive."

Dr. Jim nodded. "Yes. Prosperity is not personal. It's collective. The Kingdom grows as we give."

Then came the humor that always follows revelation.

As Mark dropped a second guitar pick onto the ground, he sighed. "Well, there goes my last excuse for not playing at Mom's potlucks."

Anna smirked. "Careful. The Kingdom might make you its music minister."

Lila pointed toward the glowing tree. "I think the choir already started without you."

Even Elena laughed, her eyes bright. "And that," she said, "is the sound of true abundance — when laughter comes easier than worry."

Dr. Jim chuckled. "Exactly. Laughter is the sound of fear losing its grip."

They laughed until the stars seemed to echo back their joy. In that moment, the whole garden shimmered brighter — as if every sound of love, every act of giving, every surrender of fear had been absorbed by the living heart of Spirit itself.

As dawn began to lighten the eastern sky, they rose to walk one last time through the garden. At the center stood a magnificent tree, its trunk wide enough to shelter them all. Upon its branches hung fruit inscribed not with words, but with names — names of friends, teachers, even strangers they had once helped without knowing.

Anna touched a branch and found her father's name there, glowing softly beside her own. "It looks like the story doesn't end here," she whispered.

Elena smiled through tears. "It never does. Love just keeps writing."

Dr. Jim placed a hand on the tree. "This is the Tree of Circulation — the living symbol of divine economy. Every gift becomes fruit for another soul. Every act of love plants another root. And so the garden grows forever."

The wind moved through the branches like a benediction.

They lingered in silence until Anna finally said, "Dr. Jim… after all this, what's the one truth you want us to carry home?"

He smiled. "That prosperity is not what you keep — it's what keeps you alive. Give your time, and you'll never feel forgotten. Share your talent, and you'll never feel small. Offer your treasure, and you'll never feel poor. When you give yourself away, you meet the part of God that can never run out."

That night, as stars bloomed fully above the Kingdom, Anna sat beside the river and opened her journal. Her heart was full beyond speech, but words — as they often do when love overflows — began to find her.

She wrote the way prayer writes itself — not from mind, but from soul.

Slam Poem
"The Kingdom of Prosperity"

They told us prosperity was gold in a vault,
Stacks in a bank, a bigger house, a higher wall.
But here's the truth whispered in light:
It's not what you keep.
It's what you release.
Time — the heartbeat you lend to another.
Talent — the spark God gave you to scatter.

Treasure — the river that flows when you trust
that giving never empties you.
It fills you.

The Kingdom isn't in the sky —
It's in the breath that says,
"Yes. I will give. Yes. I will live."
Because prosperity is not pursued — it's shared.
Not earned — but remembered.
Not found — but revealed
when love circulates through open hands.
The gates were never locked.
We just had to open our hearts.

Closing Refrain — "Lean on Me" (Adapted for Congregation)

Lean on me, and I'll lean on you,
Together we'll see what Spirit can do.
Time, Talent, Treasure — the gifts that we bring,
Open the Kingdom, and let our hearts sing.

Philosophical Meaning

Prosperity is not accumulation; it is participation. It is not a possession to protect but a rhythm to remember. The Kingdom of Prosperity is the consciousness of divine circulation — a state of trust so deep that giving and receiving merge into one holy breath.

To live prosperously is to live as a steward of divine abundance, not an owner. Emerson said, *"The law of love is the law of abundance."* Thoreau reminded us that simplicity is the secret of wealth. Holmes declared, *"Life is infinite energy, ever seeking expression."*

When you realize that you are not apart from this flow but a channel of it, you awaken to your divine inheritance: peace that doesn't run out, joy that doesn't depend on circumstance, and love that cannot be measured.

Prosperity is not someday — it is this moment, shared, multiplied, and made sacred by gratitude.

Reflective Self-Inquiry — "The Flow of the Kingdom"

Where in my life am I still trying to *own* what Spirit has only asked me to *steward?* What would it feel like to trust the flow instead of managing the outcome?

How can I give my *time* in ways that plant presence and peace in the lives of others? How might Spirit be inviting me to offer my attention more consciously?

Which *talent* within me longs to be shared, not for recognition, but for healing?

What stops me from offering it freely?

What does *treasure* mean to me — and how might generosity reshape my relationship with it?

Can I see giving not as loss, but as participation in divine abundance?

How can I practice prosperity as a *spiritual rhythm,* not a financial pursuit?

What would my life look like if I believed that love, time, and good itself are infinite?

Final Word

This is the moment of stewardship — not from guilt, not from duty, but from joy. The Kingdom of Prosperity is not a distant promise. It is here, now, waiting in every act of giving, every word of gratitude, every moment of love freely shared.

The story doesn't end here because life never stops multiplying what you give in faith.

The Kingdom is within you — and it begins the moment you open your hands.

If you like this book, get these other two books by Jim Turrell, available on Amazon.com:

Jesus Under The Hood

When it's Time to Leave

www.ingramcontent.com/pod-product-compliance
Lightning Source LLC
Chambersburg PA
CBHW061339040426
42444CB00011B/2999